HAPPINESS IS JUST A BREATH AWAY

HAPPINESS IS JUST A BREATH AWAY

How to Achieve High energy, Confidence & Vitality

KAWENA
(Gwen Gordon)

First edition 2010

National Library of Australia
Cataloguing-in-Publication entry:

Gordon, Gwen, 1928
Happiness is just a breath away :
How to achieve high energy, confidence & vitality / Kawena (Gwen Gordon).

ISBN: 978-1-921630-30-9 (pbk.)

Happiness.
Self-actualization (Psychology).
Conduct of life.

158.1

Published by Global Publishing Group
PO Box 517 Mt Evelyn, Victoria 3140 Australia
Email: info@TheGlobalPublishingGroup.com

For Further information about orders:
Phone: +61 3 9736 1156 or Fax +61 3 8648 6871

Dedicated to
Elizabeth Jane Stacey
who was my wonderful foster
mother and loving guide.

ACKNOWLEDGEMENTS

I give thanks to my daughter Elizabeth Joy for always being there with love, laughter and caring and allowing Mum to do it her own way. Also for being generous enough to share your many ideas and creative thoughts, some of which found their way into this book, so thank you for being a huge part of my life, with love Mum.

To my ex-husband Leslie – along the way you always seemed to know what positive thinking books to bring home when I ran out of them. Thank you for the happy times (and there were lots) and lessons learned in the not so happy times.

Peter my eldest son, what great conversations and understanding we had along the way and the love you gave. You too have my love and respect, you, Mary and your family have done well. I am proud of all of you.

Barry my youngest son, you were the first to accept and understand that your mother was a little different; I thank you for your support and help in those early days when I wasn't sure of myself.

It's great to see you and Delma so happy. You've come a long way.

Danny and Sally, well what can I say to my two special work-angels. You have worked tirelessly to help me, especially with my CD's and my amazing website. I am very grateful and proud to be your Gran'ma and Shai's Mamar.

I'd like to give special thanks to Darren Stephens and his team at Global Publishing Group for the great help and guidance I was given along the way.

THANKING MY HELPERS ALONG THE WAY

Crystena – who is always available whenever I need assistance, especially when I need copies of this and that. Thank you for your love, patience and care.

Karin – thank you for the wonderful exchange of conversations. Looking back I see we have both come a long way since eight years ago. Thank you for your love and support.

Robyn T – what fun we've had putting this book together. Me doing the scribble, and you doing the hard work on your computer. Thank you for some great creative ideas. I'm amazed that we finally got there.

Tracey – thank you for the complete and utter faith you have and always have had in my work and healing abilities. We've got lots more to do.

Robyn P – what fun and laughter we have tossing around new ideas and thoughts at our morning teas. They are precious times.

Trish T – You were there in the beginning, encouraging and being positive on my behalf. You always knew I would finish this project. Thank you for your love and respect.

Jean-Paul – I am very grateful for the support and respect you have shown for my work, my book and myself. For this I give you my thanks.

Ossie and Petrina – Thank you for accepting me just the way I am, and being so interested in my work and book.

Sandy R – If it hadn't been for your faith and encouragement in my abilities in the early days, I may never had made it this far. Thank you for your love.

Margie N – Remember your Creative Writing Course I joined twelve years ago? Well I have proved, "it's never too late". Much love.

CONTENTS

Acknowledgements

Preface

Introduction

Chapter 1. Happiness begins at Home –   1
            Self Respect

Chapter 2. Breathing Happiness & Energy   23
            Into Your Life

Chapter 3. The Power of Your Incredible
            Mind   75

Chapter 4. Have Fun and Dream   95

Chapter 5. The Importance of Affirmations   117

Chapter 6. Meditation and Motivation   145

Chapter 7. Loving and Gifting   169

Chapter 8. My Grateful List   219

Chapter 9: Kawena's Summing Up   223
            My Favourite Books   237
            About the Author   234

PREFACE

I met Kawena almost five years ago.

She struck me as an amazingly happy and energetic wise lady, who certainly walked her talk.

I could feel the belief in herself and her simple happiness radiated through her twinkly eyes.

I wanted to be like her! In a few minutes of a chance meeting I was on a personal happiness journey.

Kawena has fulfilled her own dream by writing this book and you will fulfil yours by becoming a much happier person if you embrace her words.

Let's fly with Kawena.

Lydia Caplygin
Group Advertising
Manager

INTRODUCTION

THIS WORKBOOK
IS WRITTEN IN A
VERY BASIC AND
SIMPLE WAY
TO HELP OTHERS
UNDERSTAND HOW TO
TAP INTO THE INCREDIBLE

POWER
OF THE UNIVERSE

BY RAISING THEIR
OWN LEVELS OF
ENERGY

AND IS A

CULMINATION
OF MY OWN
EXPERIENCES
DURING A LONG LIFETIME
80 YEARS
OF TRIAL AND ERROR
AND WALKING
MY OWN TALK.

Out of the many classes I have attended and the reading and information others have shared, I have chosen certain steps to follow and you can be sure that anything I recommend I have practised.

You see my main asset is the amount of years I have had for trial and error.

Oh yes! There have been quite a few mistakes along the way and they have been my greatest learning of all.

I was a late starter on my Spiritual Journey because there was very little information compared to these days and we had to search harder than we do now.

I was around sixty years of age when a greater awareness and deeper understanding became the way of truly living my life. I stepped out of the square and became a free spirit and decided on a path of self discovery and achievement.

This was when the fun really began and my life took on <u>a whole new meaning.</u>

My first personal awareness began the day my then husband, Les, went to the dump to get rid of some rubbish and brought home a box of brand new books. Amongst them was a book called The

Power of Positive Thinking by Norman Vincent Peale. It became my second bible and I still use one for my research today, the original finally fell apart. All this was way back in 1953 and these sorts of books were only just being written. That was what I like to call, the beginning of the information era. We were the first of the baby boomers after the Second World War and most of us were dead set on improving ourselves and our way of life.

On looking back now, I give that book credit for setting me on a path of positive thinking, wellness and happiness. After that, self worth books became a passion. I did not realize that from then on I wasn't only learning how to improve myself but that I'd be guiding others how to be the best person they possibly can be and enjoy every moment of it.

After years of positive books I sort of graduated into Spiritual awareness and Robert Schuller books guided me there.

I'm not one for organised religion but I do respect other people's choices and like many others I have my simple basic beliefs and they get me through beautifully. In my opinion freedom of choice is a wonderful thing.

The next milestone was a bit of a surprise. Elizabeth came home one day and said, "Mum I think you had better go and check the bookshop at Runaway Bay, they've got a great book and angel cards combined that might suit you."

So I went down and brought two lots didn't I? We need to remember that this was the beginning of angel awareness and now there are hundreds of wonderful angel books out there.

Of course sprinkled all through these years my passion was in attending all the classes I could find on natural healing and meditation. Life was certainly becoming very interesting.

One special thing stands out. At forty five the urge to learn to sing came to me and that taught me the value of quality breathing and became my next passion because my health improved so incredibly. I still study and research all I can on the effects and benefits of deep breathing on our bodies.

IF YOU ARE HAPPY BEING MISERABLE

THIS BOOK IS **NOT** FOR YOU.

If you are at least a little bit curious and think you might find at least one atom of help within these pages, then stay with me.

AND LET'S FLY TOGETHER.

THIS IS A PRACTICAL WORKBOOK ON CREATING YOUR OWN HAPPINESS.

My main focus is to show you some of the many natural ways I use to raise my own high energy levels, so that at eighty years of age I can still function as well as I did at forty years of age.

To me life's merry-go-round seems to be going faster and faster, even the young ones I teach say the same thing.

If you take nothing else from my book I hope you take on and learn to understand quality breathing and show others.

My main disappointment in life is that schools, doctors and others aren't making the youth conscious of breathing exercises.

So many of my past clients say that their life really turned around and they are much happier because of it.

"HAPPINESS IS JUST A BREATH AWAY"

Was originally put together with a special section of the community in mind which are the CARERS and those responsible for other's wellbeing.

These are very emotional areas to work from and can require much more energy than just looking after ourselves.

Many people have reviewed the book before it went to print and <u>NOW</u> agree it is suitable for anyone from all walks of life.

With the fast pace of life we all need much more energy to cope with than we used to. I have simply shared with you what works for me. I hope some of it will work for you.

In Summary - "It is a great Handbook"

- To inspire and motivate

- For maintaining good health and inner strength, and

- Handy to refer to when going through tough times.

*I WILL BE USING
THE WORD
GOD*

*IF IT ISN'T YOUR STYLE
SIMPLY
REPLACE IT WITH
WHATEVER
YOU ARE COMFORTABLE
WITH*

IT'S YOUR CHOICE.

Chapter 1

Happiness begins at Home – Self Respect

TRUE

SUCCESS

_IN LIFE
IS MEASURED BY
THE **LEVEL OF**
HAPPINESS
YOU CREATE
FOR YOURSELF
NO MATTER HOW
RICH OR
POOR YOU ARE.
INTERESTED IN THIS
STATEMENT?
THEN READ ON._

HAPPINESS BEGINS AT HOME

Many years ago when a teacher of self confidence told our class, "you must learn to put yourself first" I thought "how selfish is that?"

Now when I repeat that sentence to my class I get the same reaction. It seems nothing has changed. Like other helpers and self sacrificers I had to learn that if I didn't look after me, I might end up not able to help anyone – even myself.

We can end up physically, mentally and emotionally drained trying to please everyone and in the end nobody wins and you could even need help yourself.

In the end I found that as I valued myself more my confidence and self respect grew, and so can yours.

Be your own self nurturer and you'll also be able to help those around you more, and be a shining example to others.

Develop a happy, cheerful personality and you'll attract new like minded friends into your life.

One thing I have learned is that the more you learn about a given subject the more there is to learn. It is amazingly never ending.

Life's certainly interesting if we let it be.

One of my mum's favourite sayings was, "THERE IS NOTHING NEW UNDER THE SUN" and that was about sixty years ago. Even that far back her explanation was that all information is on what she called, "THE ETHER" ready for us to tap into.

Over the years I have read thousands of books, attended dozens of workshops and listened to hundreds of tapes and CD's.

In doing all this I have learned that nothing has basically changed, just added to from others and my own experiences.

I do find it quite funny that modern science in its effort to disprove our beliefs has often proved them right.

Often I pick up an old Edgar Cayce book or Napoleon Hill, Norman Vincent Peale and others and realise how timeless they are and that modern books, including my own are simply an extension of the originals written and added to for modern times.

Sometimes in my researching those books I am surprised to find what I thought was modern "lingo" already written and even explained then. There truly is nothing new under the sun.

NOW

LET'S

TURN

THE

CRAPPINESS

INTO

HAPPINESS

WE

CAN DO IT!!

THE WOW FACTOR

LET'S

GO

ALONG

THE

<u>WOW</u>

PATH

NOT THE

WOE PATH!!

IT'S TIME TO

GIVE YOURSELF

A

NEW MAKEOVER

<u>ON</u>

<u>THE</u>

<u>INSIDE</u>

THEN THE OUTSIDE
WILL LOOK AFTER ITSELF
IT'S TIME TO START.

PRACTICING
THE ART OF BEING HAPPY.

It's time to start learning to be happy while you are waiting for your dreams to fall into place, then they will come much faster that you expected.

Don't wait till you receive the million dollars – the Rolls Royce – the flash house. Practice being happy each day as it comes.

Make the effort to think yourself happy and you'll be happy with or without the goodies, and when they do come it's a great bonus.

THE GOODIES THEN, ARE JUST THE ICING ON THE CAKE!

Go to www.expandingenergies.com.au for Happiness Affirmations by Kawena

THE ART OF BEING HAPPY

IS EASY WHEN YOU KNOW HOW.

HAPPINESS

IS LIKE LEARNING THE

PIANO.

THE MORE YOU PRACTICE

*THE **BETTER** YOU GET.*

*IF WE WANT **HAPPINESS**
WE MUST **INVITE IT**
INTO OUR
LIVES.*

*WE HAVE TO PUT **THE
WELCOME MAT** OUT.*

*IT WON'T COME
OF ITS' OWN ACCORD.*

*WE NEED TO DO THE WORK
TO EARN IT, BECAUSE WE
ALONE ARE RESPONSIBLE
FOR OUR OWN HAPPINESS.*

THINKING

HAPPINESS

BRINGS HAPPINESS.

_IT'S_ **_NOT POSSIBLE_**

TO

THINK HAPPY

AND

UNHAPPY

AT THE

SAME
TIME.

www.HappinessIsJustABreathAway.com

GETTING THE HAPPINESS HABIT.

*PRACTICE BEING HAPPY
WITH THE SMALL THINGS
AND THE BIG THINGS
WILL FOLLOW.*

*THE MORE WE INSIST
ON BEING HAPPY
THE **MORE WE WILL BE**.*

*THE MORE WE INSIST
ON BEING UNHAPPY
THE **MORE WE WILL BE**.*

*IT IS ALWAYS
OUR CHOICE.*

SELF ESTEEM

IF WE ARE

TALL – SHORT – BIG – SMALL – BLACK – WHITE – OR YELLOW

ON THE OUTSIDE, IT MATTERS NOT.

Each human being is an absolutely amazing <u>original</u> creation, and we need to know what's going on in the inside. Keep yourself clean and tidy, do the best on the outside presentation then forget it and focus on what is going on internally.

When we start really getting to know ourselves amazing things start to happen on the outside. You'll find that your new enthusiasm, joy and happiness bring a special glow with them and when we learn to value that unique person we truly are, our happiness shows in our face. Also in learning to build up our own confidence and self esteem we are automatically learning how to guide others in the future when they need help. It is even more interesting when you realise you have become your own spirit lifter, and that's another WOW Factor, a real plus on your new journey forward.

WE ALL HAVE LIMITLESS POTENTIAL

It is so sad so many of us never reach it.

Also, so many of us never ever realise what our true talents are, and when we do understand what our talents are, we are too fearful to put them out there

WHAT A WASTE TO THE WORLD.

Come to <u>www.expandingenergies.com.au</u> to receive your copy of: Confidence Affirmations by Kawena

The need to encourage each other in this direction has never been more important or more available.

> *It's time to share, teach and guide others to what we have learned in a big way.*

We are fast becoming more aware of our own greatness and potential, so open up, be brave, the age of information is truly here, there is so much to hand and so many opportunities to learn and put that learning into action.

By spreading our knowledge and talents across the planet much more satisfaction and happiness comes to us.

SHARING AND CARING IS ANOTHER KEY TO HAPPINESS, IT ALWAYS HAS BEEN.

But we are now becoming more aware of our own possibilities and potential.

So open up, be bold and begin to go forward.

WE CAN DO IT; IT JUST TAKES THAT FIRST STEP.

The main thing to remember here is it's ok to make mistakes.

We were born to do just that so we can learn lessons and become strong.

*IT IS TIME TO **SLOW***
D-O-W-N
TO MEET THE REAL YOU.
SOME OF US ARE SO BUSY
RACING THROUGH
LIFE
OUR FOCUS BECOMES
BLURRED

AND OUR
SENSES BECOME
NUMBED.

SO WE DO MISS THE
WONDERFUL NATURAL
BEAUTY THAT IS WAITING
FOR US TO OBSERVE AND
TUNE INTO
ENTHUSIASM.

THE WORD **ENTHUSIASM**
COMES FROM THE GREEK
WORD **ENTHEOS** WHICH
MEANS IN GOD.

THINK WITH
ENTHUSIASM

TALK WITH ENTHUSIASM

ACT WITH ENTHUSIASM

PRACTICE LOVING YOURSELF,
YOUR LIFE AND OTHERS WITH ENTHUSIASM

SOUL

For the last fifty years I have seen spiritual information slowly filtering through and now it is reaching crescendo point which tells us that we are not on our human journey but on our soul journey.

Recognising this gives us creative power over our own lives.

I can only think of the soul as coming from our enthusiasm, passion and energy levels. The part of us that looks for the truth; the positive, the loving and the exciting part of ourselves and others. When we think about it, it makes sense when we realise the word enthusiasm is taken from the Greek word entheos which means "IN GOD." The human mind mostly tells us all the reasons why we can't follow our amazing dreams.

SPIRIT QUIETLY SAYS LET'S GO!

It's interesting to think that what we call our "higher self" is our soul connection to God.

Some of us call it the God spark within. With this new surge of spiritual and planetary energy we are becoming so eager to learn more of our soul's journey and this whole (new) concept of who and what we are, it seems the information we so crave is finally being unleashed and the understanding and excitement is building up.

It is so gratifying to see so many people in higher places tapping into this new wave of empathy and understanding eg. Governments, religions and even the rich people are sharing more than ever as they realise we are all part of each other.

> *We are finally beginning to take responsibility for our own lives and actions.*

Deep down inside I feel a quiet happiness when I hear others accepting that they are their own co-creators. With this awareness I feel

THERE IS GREAT HOPE FOR THE FUTURE.

Chapter 2

Breathing Happiness into Your Life

BREATHING

_IS_

ABSOLUTELY

THE MOST

IMPORTANT

THING

YOU WILL EVER

_DO IN_

YOUR LIFE!!

THE

BREATH

OF LIFE.

Oxygen is the <u>MAGIC MEDICINE</u> that activates and re energises every cell, nerve ending and chakra in the body.

It also revitalises our natural chemicals and immune system.

What's more, it gives us the power to focus more clearly.

AND IT'S FREE!

So it makes sense to value it and learn the deep breathing techniques.

BREATHING AND HEALING

Breathing <u>is</u> the single most important thing we'll ever do in life, and our <u>whole</u> <u>existence</u> depends on it.

Everything we say, do or think absolutely relies on our breathing abilities. Knowing this, it makes sense that if we do quality breathing and supply the body with more oxygen we will achieve a much better quality of life, and our health will improve dramatically, especially the immune system.

We need to know that the more oxygen we supply the body with, the greater our energy levels become and the more focused our minds will be.

> *By providing our body with more oxygen we are giving it the greatest healing tool on the planet.*

Every cell, muscle, ligament, tendon, tissue, gland and every other part of our bodies, especially the wheels of energy called the chakras, react to extra oxygen.

BREATHWORK

IS AN

EMPOWERING

PROCESS THAT CAN HELP
RELEASE

TENSIONS

EMOTIONS

AND

BLOCKAGES

IN BOTH THE

BODY AND THE

PSYCHE.

THE OXYGEN STORY

It wasn't until I turned about forty five that I became aware of the magic of quality breathing.

The family had all grown up and left home, and like most of us at this stage of life I felt the need deep down inside to fill the void that was left in my life.

This is a time in most of our lives where we feel a need to be creative in a different way. We go through thinking, "What will I do for the rest of my life?"

Some of us wonder "what are my talents?" And sometimes a little pity partying goes on where we feel nobody needs us anymore, and if we let it, it can be quite depressing.

However after a while I looked back at when I was very young and wondered what I would have done had I not married at an early age and then remembered my greatest desire was to sing and act.

Commonsense those days suggested it was too late to be a singer, and don't make a fool of yourself.

Those days the closest thing we had to a karaoke machine was this incredible modern machine called a tape recorder, almost obsolete now.

Wow! Was I excited.

A whole new world was about to open up. I found I could carry a tune, had good rhythm, but I wasn't overly impressed.

One day I was browsing through the local paper, yes, we did have The Bulletin then, and quite by accident an advertisement jumped right out at me, singing teacher available.

Bingo, along I trot and knocked on the door of her home and saw this very young woman, named Tricia White, standing there and almost changed my mind. However having got this far I couldn't back out.

I was very shy in those days, believe it or not, but managed to ask, "Can you teach older people how to sing?"

Laughing Tricia said, "If you can talk and breathe, I can teach you how to sing."

From then on I was to learn that the key to producing good singing and voice production relies on deep breathing and how to control it.

THAT'S NOT ALL I DISCOVERED!

After months of practicing quality breathing I found that by drawing in all that extra oxygen:

- My body began to heal itself

- My energy rose dramatically

- My mind became more focused

- And I could think more clearly.

AND ALL THIS BECAUSE I WANTED A HOBBY.

Then as usual I went searching for information. In came books on breathing and I learned heaps about oxygen and its' magic healing properties.

Looking back now I think it's amazing how well most of us cope with life while only shallow breathing. Like the old saying goes, if I only knew then what I know now. However it is true that wisdom comes with experience.

I am so happy I learned it at all or my life wouldn't be the magic it is.

THE MAGIC OF THE BREATH

Deep breathing is necessary to help us relax and still the mind. We automatically strengthen the immune system, when we draw in extra <u>OXYGEN</u> and provide our bodies with more energy to work with.

Because our brain becomes more energised with the extra <u>OXYGEN</u>, we can make clearer decisions and connect much easier with the creative side of the brain.

Even students find study and exams are a lot easier to cope with as all energy levels are higher and focus is much clearer.

OXYGEN

Fuels the energy process

FLUIDS

Protect the membranes surrounding each cell
which strengthens the immune system.

So we find that-

OXYGEN PLUS FLUIDS

Are great energisers, immune stimulants and
even anti-viral.

So once we realise that <u>OXYGEN IS THE MAGIC
MEDICINE</u> that activates and re-energises every
cell and chakra in our bodies, it makes sense
that we should value and learn to deep breathe.
Especially when unlike other medicines it <u>COST
US ABSOLUTELY NOTHING!!</u>

BELLY BREATHING

One of the best breathing exercises of all is abdominal breathing, or what is generally called belly breathing which oxygenises the whole body from top to toe.

Learn while lying down. Gently draw the breath in through the nose, filling the lungs up as you push the tummy out, hold breath to count of three; pushing the tummy out makes more room for the lungs to expand to contain more oxygen. Then push the air out through pursed lips, squeezing in the tummy muscles gently but firmly. Keep squeezing, cleansing out all stale air, viruses and micro germs. Repeat at least five times, gradually building up to ten times, morning, around noon and in the evening.

Now we have a new fresh supply of oxygen and instant calm energy flow.

Cleansing and oxygenising the lungs this way daily can help promote extremely good health and can even help relieve headaches. The body can become so full of life, energy and vitality; your motivation and confidence has the best chance ever of improving

> *Quality breathing plus a happy outlook can make life extremely exciting.*

IT'S DEFINITELY WORTH THE EFFORT, AT LEAST TRY IT FOR A MONTH.

You should be surprised at the difference it makes, stay with it for two months and even your friends will notice the difference and by then the body, mind and spirit are so happy it becomes an automatic daily exercise, one that you really look forward to.

ANOTHER VERY SIMPLE, RELAXING MEDITATION TECHNIQUE.

If ever you become giddy, <u>stop</u> immediately.

In this exercise we will be breathing in through the nose and out through the mouth.

Sit or stand straight, shoulders dropped, head balanced.

Now take a long slow, deep breath to the count of seven, hold for the count of five and let go slowly and deeply to the count of seven.

REST

If you are on your own it is even better on the out breath to make a strong sound ha-a-a-a-a-a-a-a and when you hold the breath, think to yourself:

"I am releasing all stress and tension, I am peaceful and calm."

Repeat just five or six times and you'll be amazed at how much lighter and more focused and relaxed you will be.

Come to www.expandingenergies.com.au to hear Kawena talk you through Quality Belly Breathing.

YOUR LUNGS

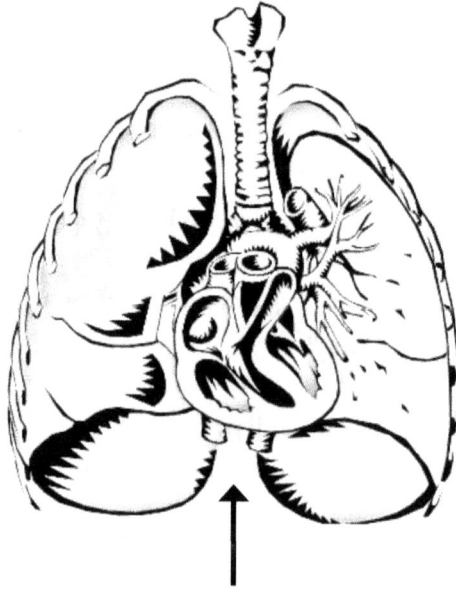

Warm moist, stale air. Breeding ground for all sorts of germs and viruses.

With shallow breathing the oxygen doesn't cleanse the bottom of the lungs.

Extra oxygen does the job and helps the immune system to be stronger.

EXPLANATION OF BELLY BREATHING

When breathing in and <u>pushing</u> the stomach out, we are allowing the lungs more <u>space</u> to <u>expand</u> and <u>fill</u> with <u>more</u> fresh air than usual.

THEN

When squeezing the stomach in to <u>expel</u> the breath, we are pushing <u>more</u> air out than usual, thus <u>cleansing</u> the lungs thoroughly of all sorts of viruses

Micro germs

Poisons and toxins.

MAKE

<u>QUALITY BREATHING</u>

YOUR <u>FIRST</u> PRIORITY

NOT THE <u>LAST</u>.

*YOU WILL FIND THAT ONCE YOU GET YOUR BODY FIRING ON **ALL** CYLINDERS*

THEN THE

MIND – BODY AND SPIRIT

*GO FULL STEAM **AHEAD** AND LIFE TAKES ON A WHOLE NEW MEANING.*

PRANIC HEALING

is available to everyone.

As the oxygen brings in energy,
the Pranic life force brings in

VITALITY

at the same time, so more nerve endings and
more cells in our body are re-energised and re-
vitalised when we practice quality breathing.

ARE YOU A STUDENT?

Then you could be amazed at how quickly the fog can clear away and your mind becomes more focused when you take on the breathing patterns, even more magical when you combine it with meditation, your whole life can turn around.

Many others including myself claim how easy study and exams become if we take on – <u>THE POWER OF BREATH.</u>

FACING OUR PROBLEMS.

Making clearer, positive choices in our lives becomes the norm, which automatically tunes us into being happier and more relaxed.

I think we really do need the support, especially at the pace we are going these days.

Looking back on my very young days we didn't need these exercises as much, because we didn't have any machines, not even a car or washing machine, we even had to use a hand mower to cut the lawn, so we were more physically active which automatically caused us to deep breathe.

THROAT BREATHING

It is worth learning to throat breathe, especially if you have ear, nose or throat trouble.

This pattern helps draw away inflammation from the head that may be building up.

Usually after a few of these breaths you will feel the need to swallow, but you will pass it through eventually. It is simply the inflammation dislodging.

I simply love throat breathing as I feel I benefit from this one more than any other. I'm sure it stops a lot of diseases and its years since I have had a cold.

Many of my clients have reported what a great thing it is to clear their sinuses and others are happy to find their headaches have disappeared.

It seems that in clearing away a lot of inflammation it takes away the pressure that builds up. Not being an MD I don't know what happens, but I do know a lot of us find relief in many areas.

YOU MIGHT LIKE TO CHECK WITH YOUR DOCTOR AND THEN GIVE IT A TRY.

PRACTICING THROAT BREATHING.

Sit comfortably straight or lie down.

Open up the lungs, shoulders (wings) back gently and close your eyes very gently.

Just breathe normally for a while and concentrate on how the air feels as it comes in through the nose.

Now with mouth closed gently, take your thoughts to the back of the throat and use the tiny muscles there to draw the breath down slowly. Then use the same muscles to gently press the air out.

Half a dozen times, twice a day can be of value.

It takes practice; some get it straight away, but don't give up, as I believe this is one of the best healing modalities available.

SILENT BODY BREATHING

This technique is extremely calming and great for settling the body and the mind in preparation for meditation.

By focusing on your breath and counting in and out you have a better chance of letting go of today's worries and cares.

If you lose count go back and start again, this way you learn to direct your thoughts and keep control.

NOW

Sit straight – shoulders (wings) gently back. Centre your head and very gently close your eyes. Relax the body completely like a rag doll. Push the shoulders down gently, then let them find their own relaxing space.

NOW

Keeping the mouth closed very gently and silently draw the breath in slowly, hold and just as SILENTLY and gently allow the breath to subside. Again draw in SILENTLY long and gentle – this time hold the breath to count of five and SILENTLY let go slowly.

This time just as quietly draw in counting slowly to 5 – hold to 5 – let go to 5.

Repeat six more times.

By now you should feel extremely calm and serene.

The exercise is very good to help us gain mind control for study and general focused thinking. It can also guide us into the sleeping state or meditation.

Come to www.expandingenergies.com.au to hear Kawena talk you through Silent Body Breathing.

FAVOURITE BREATHINGS

1. BELLY BREATHING - consists of extending the stomach to make way for the lungs to expand and allow more oxygen to fill them up.

2. THROAT BREATHING - to clear inflammation from the ears, nose and throat. Draw breath down from the nose using the tiny muscles at the back of the throat. Squeeze the breath out using those same muscles.

3. POWER BREATHING - for a great burst of energy, drawn through pursed lips and pushed out strongly through pursed lips.

4. SILENT BODY BREATHING - relaxes the body and calms the mind. Best done before meditation or resting. Draw the breath gently and soundlessly through the nose and allow it to lightly and soundlessly flow gently out through the mouth.

QUALITY BREATHING

Quality breathing will give us a far better quality of life.

Deep breathing releases endorphins and hormones to heal the immune system, strengthens the body's chemicals, balances the chakras and cleanses the aura. It also helps us think clearer, all this, just by simply focussing on our breathing abilities.

Not a large price to pay.

For those who don't like exercising (like me) you can even do them lying down.

Once you get the breathing habit your body will let you know when it wants even more.

Don't think that deep breathing will keep you awake. No, just the opposite. It brings in a powerful but calming energy as the body accepts it has got more than enough energy to keep on functioning and healing itself throughout the night.

We need to always remember that the body works twenty four hours a day and sometimes needs extra calming energy to get through the night.

Deep breathing is one of the greatest answers to a sleepless night ever. About 10-15 long, slow, silent deep breaths could really do the trick. Just feel it as the breath comes in through the body.

A I R

IS THE FOOD THE

CREATIVE SOURCE

PROVIDES FOR THE

LUNGS

TO

ELECTRIFY

THE **BODY.**

BREATH IS THE KEY

to our soul journey

while we reside

on mother earth.

It is the key to:

Our spiritual energy

Our soul energy

Our physical energy.

I believe that the more quality of breath we give ourselves the more positive is our soul's journey and the higher our connection to the creator.

Healers and psychic readers especially need to know the more focus they give the breath the more focused and clearer the mind becomes, and lifts us to that higher level we need for our connection.

As we breathe better health into our bodies we heal and become more comfortable, and without pain we think a whole lot clearer.

When our mental energy is focused on containing the pain the mind becomes foggy and it's much harder to cope with life.

It takes <u>enormous</u> energy to rise above pain, and then of course, there is not much left for the body to heal itself.

So it does make sense to realise, extra oxygen and pranic vitality is the simple answer to most of our physical, mental and spiritual health.

Get to know your own breathing system: value it, appreciate it and look after it.

IT'S THE ONLY ONE YOU HAVE THIS TIME AROUND.

OXYGEN STARVATION

CAN LEAD TO HEART ATTACK, DISEASE, EPILEPSY AND MANY OTHER INTERNAL DISORDERS.

LEARN TO BREATHE

PROPERLY AND MANY DISEASES CAN DISAPPEAR.

Many lives could be healthier and more productive if taught to simply breathe properly. There is an epidemic of aches, pains and general fatigue.

Oxygen is the link to good health and happiness.

SO TO KEEP UP THE MODERN PACE IN LIFE WE DO NEED MORE OXYGEN THAN EVER.

SPECIAL TIMES TO TAKE IN MORE FUEL FOR THE MIND AND BODY.

- FACING UP TO CONFRONTATION.

- BEFORE MAKING A BIG DECISION.

- BEFORE THAT JOB INTERVIEW.

- BEFORE AN OPERATION.

- BEFORE THAT IMPORTANT EXAM.

Plus many other situations.

Even the knowledge you are finally doing something to help yourself brings in new confidence and self esteem.

It's all worth a try; you've got nothing to lose, and everything to win.

OXYGEN

_IN GIVING THE
BODY MORE **OXYGEN**
YOU ARE GIVING IT
THE **POWER**
TO **HEAL – ENERGISE** AND
REPAIR ITSELF._

_THE SIMPLE ACT OF QUALITY
BREATHING CAN HELP YOU BE
THAT **INCREDIBLE PERSON**
YOU WERE
TRULY MEANT TO BE
WHY NOT GIVE YOUR BODY THE
POWER TO HELP YOU_

**_CREATE A WONDERFUL
NEW YOU!!_**

STRESS

WHEN IN **STRESSFUL SITUATIONS**

BREATHE IN POWERFULLY
SEVERAL TIMES

TO BRING **OXYGEN**

QUICKLY

TO THE **BRAIN**

THEN THE MIND CAN RISE
ABOVE THE EMOTIONS

AND YOU WILL HAVE

POWER

OVER THE

SITUATION.

WE ARE RECHARGING OUR BODY BATTERIES TO GO FULL STEAM AHEAD WITH FAR MORE ENERGY,

FAR MORE ENTHUSIASM, FAR MORE

CREATIVENESS,

FAR MORE PERSONAL POWER.

To improve:
- ourselves,
- our surroundings and
- our creative awareness.

Help your body do its best and give it the respect it really needs. We are truly breathing new life into our lives.

WE REALLY SHOULD BE

ASHAMED

OF

OURSELVES

BECAUSE MOST OF US

LOOK AFTER OUR **CAR'S BODY** AND **ENGINE**

FAR BETTER THAN WE

LOOK AFTER OUR OWN **BODY** AND **ENGINE.**

THE BODY NEEDS

OXYGEN AND WATER

QUALITY FOOD, REST AND EXERCISE.

THE MIND NEEDS

QUALITY THOUGHTS

WISE DECISIONS

POSITIVE ATTITUDE

CALMING MEDITATION.

THE SPIRIT NEEDS

SIMPLE TRUST

FAITH

LOVE

FUN.

BREATHING

AS YOU BREATHE IN

DEEPLY

KNOW YOU

ARE FILLING YOURSELF

*WITH **PURE ENERGY***

*AND **GOOD HEALTH***

AS YOU BREATHE OUT

***FULLY,** KNOW YOU ARE*

***LETTING GO** OF*

POISONS, TOXINS

*AND **TENSION**.*

JUST A WORD OR TWO TO CORPORATE, HIGH POWERED BUSINESS PEOPLE.

I hear you say, "I don't need more oxygen. I managed to get this far under my own steam."

Well I have news for you. Like it or not we all keep getting older and that's great, but the older we become the more important it is to keep your mind, body and spirit even stronger.

So if you want to stay at the top, stay strong, well and highly energised, then it might be a good idea to think what the power of the breath can do for you.

I often think that, what busy people call stress and tension, that leads to burn-out, is simply lack of extra oxygen to cope with the over load.

GIVE IT A TRY, YOU COULD POSSIBLY, BE VERY SURPRISED.

WITH EVERYDAY

SHALLOW BREATHING

WE ARE USING

LESS THAN

½ THE **OXYGEN**

WE HAVE **ACCESS** TO

SO IT STANDS TO REASON

WE ONLY FUNCTION

½ AS WELL AS WE COULD.

BE **_AWARE_** OF
SHALLOW
BREATHING
THIS IS WHAT CAUSES A LOT
OF **_DISEASES_**
AND
RESPIRATORY PROBLEMS.
OXYGEN
PLUS **_FLUIDS_** ARE THE
ANSWER TO 95% OF THESE
PROBLEMS, AND IT'S UP TO
US TO WORK AT IT. THEN IT
BECOMES EASY, AND OUR
TRUE HEALING
BEGINS.

GOOD BREATHING IS THE MOST EFFECTIVE WAY EVER CONCEIVED TO CONTROL FEELINGS OF STRESS AND ANXIETY.

QUALITY

BREATHING

AND

MEDITATION

ARE THE TWO

MOST VALUABLE

INVESTMENTS

OF YOUR TIME

YOU CAN EVER

MAKE

IN YOUR LIFE.

MAKE
QUALITY BREATHING
YOUR **FIRST** PRIORITY
NOT THE **LAST**.
YOU WILL FIND THAT ONCE
YOU GET YOUR BODY
FIRING ON **ALL** CYLINDERS
THEN THE
MIND, BODY
AND **SPIRIT**
GO FULL STEAM
AHEAD
AND LIFE TAKES ON
A WHOLE NEW MEANING.

GETTING TO KNOW YOUR BODY

Our bodies are incredible beings.

They are the most wonderful structures on the planet. Think of the lungs and the amazing job they do keeping us alive. Then think about the heart ticking away twenty four seven and don't forget the digestion and elimination systems working nonstop on our behalf. We are even specially constructed to connect and heal ourselves and help heal others.

Yes we certainly have a lot to be grateful for and we don't have to know it all.

JUST SIMPLY APPRECIATE OUR OWN MAGNIFICENCE AND GET ON WITH LIFE.

BE A **FRIEND**
TO YOUR BODY
NOT AN **ENEMY**:
YOU **ARE** THE
CO-CREATOR
OF AN INCREDIBLE
WALKING – TALKING
MIRACLE
YOU HAVE THE CHOICE OF
WHETHER
TO MAKE YOURSELF
HAPPY OR **MISERABLE**
SO
WHY WOULD YOU CHOOSE
THE
SECOND ALTERNATIVE?

TEAM WORK WITH YOUR BODY.

Do your share to help and it could say "thank you very much" by paying you back with good health.

Neglect it and it will pay you out with stress and tension.

Keep on neglecting it and it could turn that stress into poisons and toxins, thus lowering the immune system and creating illness.

*BECAUSE WE DON'T **EARN** OR **PAY** FOR IT*

WE TAKE OUR BREATHING ABILITY

*FOR GRANTED, AND DON'T **MAKE THE MOST OF IT.***

*DO **MOST** BREATHING THROUGH THE **NOSE***

THIS WAY

THE AIR IS FILTERED, MOISTENED AND WARMED

TO THE BODY'S TEMPERATURE THUS WE AVOID MOST GERMS

AND A DRY THROAT.

OXYGEN IS FUEL FOR THE MIND AND BODY.

Unlike today's petrol it costs nothing but thought and effort.

Don't let your body run out of fuel as your performance will suffer.

Happiness can be obtained without breathing exercises but it can be ten times better if we make the effort.

Unlike physical exercises you can do your breathing techniques anywhere. Even at the lights when you are driving or at the checkout in the supermarkets. It not only releases the tension but time flies.

You can even do it in bed with the silent breathing pattern. Your partner won't even wake up; you can do it in class, in company, even at the ball game. Yes the light breathing comes in very handy when your energy takes a dive, sometimes about two in the afternoon top up with a few extra deep breaths and away you go.

DO THE WORK

And in about a month you should feel your energy, passion and health improving in a big way.

HOWEVER IT'S ALL UP TO YOU!!

VEGETARIANISM

I became a vegetarian when I was around forty five years old.

Then it wasn't some grandiose idea of saving the animals or what I now know as absorbing poisons, toxins and anxiety from the death of animals.

No! I was just too lazy to cook different meals for the family and when my son Barry wanted to try it we all had to try it.

So in came the vegies, fruit, nuts, beans etc for six months.

When we first started I thought I might get very sick not eating meat or that I might even die. The only thing I knew then about nutrition was the little info I could find in my precious books.

However none of us got sick and none of us died.

The whole family (especially Barry) couldn't wait to get back into eating meat again EXCEPT ME.

I noticed I had never felt so well in all my life and much as I still didn't want to cook separate meals from that day to now I have not been able to get one mouthful of meat past my lips.

The only thing I do miss sometimes is fish. That was my favourite food.

I am not trying to guide anyone into being a vegetarian, just explaining what suits me. If you are curious you might like to try for six months, but be aware and make sure you get a balanced diet with plenty of protein.

Chapter 3

The Power of your Incredible Mind

WE DON'T
REALISE *WHAT POWER*
WE HAVE DEEP DOWN INSIDE.

WE DON'T
REALISE *WHAT*
WONDERFUL
THOUGHT POWER WE ARE
WASTING
BY NOT LEARNING TO
FOCUS OUR INCREDIBLE MINDS.

WE DON'T
REALISE *WHAT*
ABSOLUTELY
WONDERFUL POTENTIAL EACH
AND EVERY ONE OF US HAS
STORED DEEP DOWN INSIDE OUR
TRUE ESSENCE.

IF WE CONSTANTLY
*GIVE OUR **SUBCONSCIOUS POSITIVE MESSAGES***
*IT WILL DO IT'S BEST TO HELP US BE **HAPPY***
*AND **MOTIVATED.***

*LIKEWISE IF WE GIVE IT **NEGATIVE MESSAGES***
*IT WILL HELP US BE **MISERABLE** AND **DEPRESSED.***

START NOW!
YOU ARE THE
MASTER
OF YOUR
THOUGHTS.

THINK POSITIVE
AND YOUR
VISION
WILL BECOME
YOUR LIFE.

AS WE THINK OUR
THOUGHTS
THEY MERGE INTO THE
UNIVERSE.

*WE LEARN TO **LIVE**
WHEN
WE **LIVE** TO **LEARN**.*

*OUR PRESENT
THINKING SHAPES
OUR **FUTURE**.*

*IT CAN CREATE A LIFE OF
NEGATIVE PAIN*

OR

*IT CAN CREATE A LIFE OF
INCREDIBLE HAPPINESS.*

SAY TO YOURSELF:
I AM MOULDING MY
LIFE
BY THE
IMPRINTS

I PLACE IN MY
SUBCONSCIOUS.

MY **LIFE** *IS SIMPLY A*
REFLECTION *OF MY*
THOUGHTS
I PLACE THEM
WISELY.

WE

NEED

TO

*DWELL ON THE **POSITIVE***

NOT

*THE **NEGATIVE** THINKING.*

*WE **ARE***

THE RESULTS OF

OUR OWN

PROGRAMMING

***START** CREATING*

A WONDERFUL

NEW PLAN

AND YOU WILL CREATE

A

WHOLE

NEW

YOU!

THE
SUBCONSCIOUS MIND

IS OUR

SILENT PARTNER
IT FORGETS
NOTHING

AND WORKS FOR US 24 HOURS A DAY.

SO
ALWAYS GIVE IT
THE BEST POSSIBLE
INFORMATION
YOU CAN.

THE MORE WE

RELAX** THE **MIND

THE DEEPER

*WE **CONNECT***

*WITH THE **SOUL**.*

NO MATTER WHAT

NOBODY

CAN TAKE AWAY

OUR

SOUL OR **SPIRIT**.

HOW **WE THINK** IN OUR HEADS IS **OUR BUSINESS** AND **NOBODY ELSE'S**.

THIS IS WHERE OUR TRUE CHOICES IN LIFE ARE.

HOW AND WHAT WE

THINK.

I
LOVE
THIS
ONE...

THE <u>SUBCONSCIOUS MIND</u>

IS LIKE A **<u>RECORDING</u>**

IT REPRODUCES WHATEVER **<u>YOU IMPRESS</u>** *ON IT.*

FROM THE BOOK:

"THE MIRACLE OF THE MIND DYNAMICS"

BY JOSEPH MURPHY

*TEAMWORK
WITH THE BODY, MIND
AND SPIRIT*

*WILL TURN AN EXTRA
ORDINARY PERSON INTO
A SUPER EXTRA ORDINARY
PERSON.*

*LISTEN TO YOUR BODY
LISTEN TO YOUR MIND
LISTEN TO YOUR SPIRIT*

*AND DO WHAT IT TAKES TO
GIVE THEM WHAT THEY NEED.*

THE
SUBCONSCIOUS MIND
IS OUR
SILENT PARTNER
IT FORGETS
NOTHING
AND WORKS FOR US 24 HOURS A DAY
SO
ALWAYS GIVE IT THE
BEST POSSIBLE
INFORMATION
YOU CAN.

THE SUBCONSCIOUS MIND

Our DIVINE INTELLIGENCE lives within the SUBCONSCIOUS MIND.

It can REVEAL EVERYTHING we want to KNOW!

Feed it POSITIVE INFORMATION so it can help you ACHIEVE your hearts desires.

TAKE CHARGE, be HONEST, be STRONG.

Our SUBCONSCIOUS MIND BELIEVES what we THINK and FEED IT and FOLLOWS through WITHOUT QUESTION.

The SUBCONSCIOUS NEEDS SLEEP to RECHARGE.

Each day we are GIVEN a new lot of ENERGY.

USE IT WISELY

FAKE IT
TILL YOU
MAKE IT.

IF YOU AREN'T ALREADY A POSITIVE THINKER, TURN IT AROUND BY HAVING A
GAME OF PRETEND WITH LIFE.

PRETEND YOU ARE HAPPY EVEN WHEN YOU'RE NOT KEEP IT FUN TILL IT BECOMES YOUR REALITY

THEN YOU'LL REALLY FLY.

OUR
TIME ON THE
PLANET
IS VERY *IMPORTANT.*

<u>USE IT WISELY</u>

ONE OF THE
BIGGEST JOBS
WE NEED TO DO ON
EARTH
IS TO KEEP ON
CLEANING UP THE
CLUTTER IN OUR MINDS
AS WE GO ALONG.

INSPIRATION

DEDICATION

AND

MOTIVATION

WILL MAKE ANY

DREAM COME TRUE.

CONFUCIUS SAYS:

TELL ME
I FORGET

SHOW ME
I LEARN

INVOLVE ME
I UNDERSTAND.

BEING YOUR
OWN
CO-CREATOR
MEANS BEING GUIDE
AND TEACHER TO
YOUR OWN
SOUL
USING THE POWER OF
YOUR MIND
CONNECTED TO THE
UNIVERSAL SOURCE
COMBINED WITH THE
LOVE IN YOUR HEART.

Chapter 4

Have Fun and Dream

DON'T DREAM YOUR LIFE AWAY –
IT'S TIME TO GET OFF YOUR BACKSIDE
AND DO SOMETHING ABOUT IT OR ALL YOU WILL END UP WITH IS
A LIFETIME OF DREAMS.

Always remember the old saying 'beginning's half done' and when the universe knows you mean business it swings into action too and starts sending you the tools to follow your dream. Don't be concerned about how your dream is achieved, just set it in motion.

Even just buying a book on the subject is simply showing you have the faith, you can have that dream.

I often hear others saying (and in the past so have I): "When the time is right I'll do it". It's most unlikely that you will.

Then I hear others saying, "I can't afford it, I

haven't got the connections I need, I'm not highly educated, I haven't got this and I haven't got that, etc."

Then you need to show your faith and trust that once you start, these things can fall into place because until you show you are willing to take a risk why should the universe work in with you by sending what you need?

Never look too far ahead, just do what you can towards this wonderful dream as you go along, because believe me it usually ends up very different and often even better.

> *Having dreams is great because they stimulate our imagination and we grow and go forward on our earthly journey, becoming stronger and more creative.*

When you start stirring up the creative side of the brain it's wise to carry a pen and pad at all times, even put one next to the bed because no matter how simple your creative thought is you most likely will forget it.

I have found relaxing under the shower often triggers a bright idea, so leave a pen and pad in the bathroom too.

The main times you'll be a receiver of creative messages is when you are in a peaceful situation, as your guides never deliver messages or guidance when your mind is in a messy, screwed up condition.

Don't be surprised if you are woken at 3am, make sure you write it down because no matter how much you think you'll remember it in the morning you very seldom do and you might lose a very valuable idea.

Keep it light and even fun on the way and you will draw to you what you need, keep positive and aim high. Don't expect to be able to do it all by yourself, be brave and ask for help when you need it and don't be afraid to delegate, but be discerning who you involve in your project.

At this point always follow your gut feeling as this sensing is your soul warning you which way to go.

If you feel good about a situation then jump in the deep end and swim like mad.

If you feel a dark over-whelming sense of foreboding don't even put your toe in the water, drop the situation and run like mad.

SOMEONE
DUMPING ON YOU?
CRITICISING YOU?

DON'T TAKE IT ON.

USE

YOUR INNER WISDOM

TO UNDERSTAND THAT THEY ARE
HURTING INSIDE MORE THAN YOU
ARE, OTHER-WISE THEY WOULDN'T
DREAM OF HURTING OTHERS.
SEND THEM LOVE AND BLESSINGS,
AND LET IT GO.

UPSET?

I've learned that one of the best things to do on life's journeys is when something extremely upsetting comes into your life it's ok to let go and get angry for a little while.

Then face up to it – let go of the crappy stuff as you go along, then it won't stick to you and accumulate.

Let's be real and understand that for everyone on the planet;

THE RHYTHM OF LIFE IS THAT WE HAVE SOME GOOD AND SOME BAD, AND HOW WE FACE UP TO THE NOT SO GOOD BRINGS US OUR

STRENGTH

AND

WISDOM.

My greatest saving grace is to remember what my mum used to say when I was unhappy,

"There's always someone worse off than you."

LET'S TURN YOUR NEGATIVE STORY INTO A POSITIVE ONE

LOST YOUR JOB?

LOST THE LOVE OF YOUR LIFE?

LIFE SUCKS?

SEEMS TO BE NO HOPE?

Don't despair. You've got a brand new slate to work with for a_BRAND_NEW_BEGINNING and do you know what? You are in company with MILLIONS_OF_OTHERS and if we've got one ounce of guts, we pick ourselves up, get angry, get over it and GET ON WITH IT.

> *No more pity partying*

TIME IS OF THE ESSENCE use it wisely.

This is absolutely a new day. Start your new journey now.

There's never been a better time to start doing it your way.

Even if it means simply, going to the library to borrow a book on the subject of your new interest.

As they say "once you are at the bottom of the ladder the only way is up."

FEELING SORRY FOR YOURSELF?

OK GUYS
NO MORE
PITY PARTYING.
BELIEVE ME
LIFE'S TOO SHORT.

SO NO MATTER HOW BAD IT IS...

* GET ANGRY
* WORK THROUGH IT
* GET OVER IT
* AND GET ON WITH IT
BEFORE YOU STUFF IT UP ALL
TOGETHER.

But we will need a lot of patience, soul searching and effort.

I know that this part of the book seems pretty tough and daunting but once we start looking forward and creating our own happiness just imagine how much we are lifting our spirit and how much lighter our soul feels.

Even our physical body reacts and begins its own new journey of self healing.

The biggest deal of all is that through the power of your amazing mind you have taken on the responsibility for your own happiness and have truly become your own co-creator.

If you would like a private session with Kawena to help create a new direction, inspiration or motivation in your life go to: <u>www. expandingenergies.com.au</u>

Click on Sessions Info

SELF PITY
DRAINS OUR
ENERGY,
PULLS US DOWN
AND TAKES
AWAY OUR DREAMS,
IT UNDERMINES
ALL OUR SELF ESTEEM AND
CONFIDENCE.

<u>Don't</u> let it happen to you.

<u>Don't</u> let it become a habit.

<u>Do</u> make your mind up right <u>now</u> not to fall into the SELF PITY HABIT!!

So often does a negative situation lead us to a success we might not have had otherwise.

To me life is a series of challenges and the way we face them gives us the strength to be successful as a person and an example for others to learn from.

WE
CAN
ALL

GO FAR BEYOND
WHERE WE ARE
RIGHT NOW.

CREATE **FUN**
IN YOUR LIFE.

BE THE BEST!

ABSOLUTELY
THE BEST

*PERSON YOU CAN
POSSIBLY BE.*

*DARE TO BE **LARGER**
THAN LIFE
GET EXCITED ABOUT
LIFE.*

=YOURS=

THE ENERGY OF
BEING HAPPY

CREATES A LIGHTER VIBRATION, AND DRAWS TO US
THE GOOD STUFF.

THE ENERGY OF
BEING UNHAPPY

CREATES A HEAVIER VIBRATION AND DRAWS TO US
THE NOT SO GOOD STUFF.

WE ARE CONSTANTLY IN OUR OWN COMPANY.

We are with ourselves twenty four hours a day, seven days a week. Because of that we need to work at being our own best friend, not our own worst enemy.

Praise is the key to our subconscious mind in regards to our confidence and self esteem.

It's time to turn around some of the old sayings like, 'self praise is no recommendation.'

We seem to praise others more easily than ourselves, but unless we learn to lift our own spirit by appreciating our own good qualities and down grading our negative points, then we can't be of service in a really loving way to either ourselves or others.

We are so quick to self criticise and it only takes an instant to self-destruct.

The word PRAISE simply means to commend.

We are all GOD'S DIAMONDS and he is constantly sending us the tools to polish that diamond so it will sparkle and shine.

It seems to me that if God loves us so much it's up to us to respect and love ourselves too from this day on.

*DON'T WORRY ABOUT WHAT YOU **CAN'T** DO,*

__FOCUS__

*ON WHAT YOU **CAN** DO.*

*DON'T WORRY ABOUT WHAT YOU **HAVEN'T** GOT*

__FOCUS__

*ON WHAT YOU **HAVE** GOT.*

IF WE DON'T
TEACH
WHAT
WE
LEARN
WE STIFLE THE
RHYTHM
OF
LIFE.

THIS MEANS IT'S A PRIVILEGE AND A GIFT TO BE WILLING TO PASS ON YOUR KNOWLEDGE IN YOUR OWN LIFETIME.

By spreading our knowledge and talents across the planet much more satisfaction and happiness comes to us.

SHARING AND CARING IS ANOTHER KEY TO HAPPINESS, IT ALWAYS HAS BEEN.

But we are now becoming more aware of our own possibilities and potential.

So open up, be bold and begin to go forward.

WE CAN DO IT; IT JUST TAKES THAT FIRST STEP.

The main thing to remember here is it's ok to make mistakes.

We were born to do just that so we can learn lessons and become strong.

KARMA
IF WE BELIEVE IN
BAD KARMA
THEN WE NEED TO BELIEVE IN
GOOD KARMA

THE LAW OF THE UNIVERSE ALWAYS WAS - STILL IS - AND ALWAYS WILL BE
SET IN STONE

WE ARE ALL STARTING TO REALISE THAT WHAT WE PUT OUT ALWAYS FINDS ITS WAY BACK TO US NO MATTER WHAT.

SO IT MAKES SENSE THAT IF WE PUT OUT THE GOOD STUFF WE WILL SOON GET IT BACK BUT IF WE PUT OUT THE BAD STUFF WE'LL GET THAT BACK TOO.

IT'S YOUR CHOICE!!

IT IS AS SIMPLE AS THAT.

Chapter 5

The Importance of Affirmations

When I became fully aware of the need to change my negative thoughts to positive thoughts, I found it quite a chore and constantly slipped back into the old way of thinking, but after a while I challenged myself and decided I'd turn it into a game. I don't know when it became an automatic thing to do but after a while it was quite a bit of fun. Then it turned into a habit and now I do it almost without thought.

The word affirmation wasn't used then we used to call them "sayings" and I will admit some of my mum's old sayings were quite weird, but mostly very good.

Way back when I was a young girl she had a beautiful round box sitting on the old sideboard (cupboard).

It was called a PROMISE BOX and tied to it was a nail on a pretty pink ribbon.

Inside the box was a cardboard cut out resembling a round honeycomb shape. Inside each hole was a small rolled up paper with a message typed onto it. You took up the nail and pulled the message out, unfurled it, read it, then rolled it back around the nail and placed it back into the box.

Those days it was usually a promise from the bible.

Something like "seek and ye shall find." I thought they were great.

It didn't take much to amuse us in those days, and I think that led me onto my positive path.

Another thing about replacing negative thoughts with the positive is we gain more power over our general thinking and teaches us control of our minds in any given situation, and we become much happier.

YES

*AFFIRMATIONS
AND AWARENESS
STATEMENTS DO PLAY
A BIG PART IN OUR LIVES
IF – WE – LET – THEM*

OLD HABITS DIE HARD

A very old saying, but there's another one that says, "Beginning's half done" and they are both true. The hardest part of changing bad habits IS making our minds up when to start, and if we really want to. Once we determine to go ahead it becomes easier and easier and we mostly surprise ourselves what a difference each change can make to our lives.

The real secret to change is keeping at it and at it, constantly moving forward and being determined to achieve our goal.

Another thing is don't worry or feel guilty if you slip back occasionally, just have a little growl at yourself and start again.

Remembering when you did well rather than when you didn't. You know by now the subconscious is on your side. It wants to help all it can, so feed it more positive thoughts than EVER and help it do its' job.

I don't think it pays to change more than two habits at the same time.

I suggest those 1st two could be positive thinking and quality breathing. Of course if you are already doing these two you can choose any others to suit yourself.

A FIVE MINUTE AFFIRMATION MEDITATION

Make yourself comfortable and keep very still. Gently close your eyes and slowly breathe deep down into your heart and soul.

In your mind think to yourself:

"I REALLY – REALLY CARE FOR YOU."

Now sit quietly feeling the loving calmness flow into your soul bringing a wonderful sense of peace and contentment and feeling the ebb and flow of your quiet breathing, again slowly breathe deeply down into your heart and soul and say to yourself with steady conviction:

"I AM REALLY – REALLY HAPPY."

And feel a gentle, joyful feeling touch your heart in a beautiful way. Stay and enjoy the rhythm of your breath. Go back and repeat 3 times.

The aim of this style of meditation is to place messages of self-esteem into your subconscious mind to gradually bring self confidence and inner strength back into your life; you may not believe these messages at first but do it at least once a day or even when you have a quiet moment to spare.

In one month you will have sown the seeds of these positive affirmations into your subconscious mind at least one hundred and twenty times. It's all up to you.

Here are some more affirmations you might like to use, choose which ever you need at the time -

I AM LOVE

I AM HEALTH

I AM SERVICE

I AM ABUNDANCE

I AM WISDOM

I AM WORTHY

This won't be easy to do at first but keep at it and you can win.

When you wake in the morning and you feel dreadful, tell yourself, "I feel great!" You don't have to believe it, just say it silently or out loud several times a day.

The simplicity of it all is most of us already know the subconscious moves heaven and earth to bring us what we want so if you keep putting positive words in place of negatives, in the end you can win.

It's the same with everything you want. For years now I have been guiding my meditation group to breathe into positive thoughts such as "I am health", "I am love", "I am abundance", "I am service", etc. Most of us have had some amazing results, especially those who kept it going daily.

Patience is the key, keep at it till the universe delivers, sometimes in some very unusual ways, ways you would never dream of.

Don't look on this game of life as a chore. Keep looking forward and really having fun as you create a new you and only expecting the best.

Of course there will always be a glitch now and then, but in the end you'll find out with your new way of looking at things that the good outweighs the bad and that life can become an incredible game.

ANOTHER FAVOURITE SAYING-

*TO
CHANGE
ONE'S
LIFE*

*"START IMMEDIATELY.
DO IT FLAMBOYANTLY.
WITH NO EXCEPTIONS.
(NO EXCUSES)"*

AUTHOR- WILLIAM JAMES.

*AFFIRMATIONS
ARE SIMPLE
BUT
EXTREMELY POWERFUL
PRAYERS
WHERE WE ARE
AFFIRMING
POSITIVE THOUGHTS
TO OURSELVES AND THE
UNIVERSAL SOURCE.*

ALL
AFFIRMATIONS
TO BE
THOUGHT
OR
SAID
*WITH **FULL** ON*
ENERGY.

NO WISHY WASHY
HERE
THANK YOU

SEEDING THE GARDEN OF YOUR MIND.

AFFIRMATIONS WORK

because they are your instructions to the subconscious mind to make things happen.

The subconscious does what it is told, and we have the freedom of choice of what we put there.

Train your subconscious, you be in control of what you feed into it.

Plant positive seeds, not negative seeds, into the garden of your mind.

Be strong with the energy of your words, again, don't be WISHY WASHY.

Take back your power, it's time to stand up and be counted. YOU CAN DO IT!!

MY
FAVOURITE
AFFIRMATION *IS*

EVERY
DAY IN EVERY
POSITIVE *WAY*

I AM
BETTER,
BETTER AND
BETTER

This is an old affirmation, Quoted by Emile Coue. The original saying did not have the word positive. One day at the end of a meditation, the thought popped in that we can even be better and better at being negative. So now I always include that extra word, positive.

A FEW POSITIVE AFFIRMATIONS TO HELP YOU KEEP GOING FORWARD CHOOSE THE ONE YOU NEED AT THE TIME

Constant repetition can help keep your mind flexible, active and pointed in the right direction.

I NOW CHOOSE TO BE HAPPY, IT IS MY BIRTHRIGHT.

*I HAVE RESPECT FOR EACH
AND EVERYONE'S JOURNEY,
MINE INCLUDED.*

*I BELIEVE IN MIRACLES
BECAUSE
I AM ONE.*

I TRUST MY INTUITION AND MY SENSES, THEY LEAD ME FORWARD ON MY POSITIVE JOURNEY.

I NOW HAVE THE COURAGE TO BELIEVE IN MYSELF.

FROM THIS MOMENT ON

I WILL NOT WASTE

TODAY'S ENERGY

ON THE

NEGATIVES IN MY PAST.

I WILL USE MY

GIFT OF TODAY WISELY.

I WILL PRACTICE BEING AS

HAPPY AS POSSIBLE.

FROM TODAY ON I WILL

SPEND MORE TIME WITH

MOTHER NATURE

AND FIND THE

PEACE WITHIN.

EACH DAY I FEEL MY

ENERGY, PASSION

AND HEALTH

IMPROVING IN A BIG WAY.

PLACING

AFFIRMATIONS

AROUND THE HOME IS GREAT.

EVEN IF WE END UP NOT FOCUSING
ON THEM, THE

WORDS SINK INTO THE
SUBCONSCIOUS MIND,

SUBLIMINALLY.

ANOTHER BENEFIT IS, THEY CAN HELP
OTHERS WHO

LIVE WITH

OR

VISIT YOU.

FOCUSING

TO CREATE A HAPPY – PASSIONATE – REWARDING LIFE

WRITE DOWN ON PAPER

I am training myself to receive good ideas and creative thoughts.

I am aware and focussed on what is going on around me.

I am using my sensing and feeling for what is good for my mind, body and soul.

You can also write positive affirmations for what you DESIRE.

IMAGINATION

TAKE ADVANTAGE OF THAT WONDERFUL IMAGINATION

YOU WERE BORN WITH

GIVE IT FULL REIGN.

IT WILL HELP YOU BE WHATEVER YOU WANT TO BE.
SOW THE BEST PERSONAL

AFFIRMATION SEEDS

YOU POSSIBLY CAN IN THE GARDEN OF YOUR MIND.

DO THE WORK AND YOU'LL GET YOUR REWARDS

ALWAYS SAY OR THINK YOUR

AFFIRMATIONS FULLY FOCUSED.

AND STRONGLY SO YOU IMPRINT THEM FIRMLY ON THE

SUBCONSCIOUS MIND.

THE LAST REMINDER

Always remember my two most positive and beneficial affirmations are:

No. 1

EVERY DAY
IN EVERY POSITIVE WAY
I AM BETTER –
BETTER –
AND BETTER

No. 2

I FEEL WELL
I FEEL WONDERFUL
I FEEL GREAT

Both to be said or thought at least when you first get up, when you go to bed, and several times daily, and said strongly.

With the second affirmation the more we feel like something the cat dragged in overnight the more we need to focus on the words whether you believe them or not.

DO THE WORK

And in about a month you should feel your energy, passion and health improving in a big way.

HOWEVER IT'S ALL UP TO YOU!!

Chapter 6

Meditation and Motivation

MEDITATION

_IS_

A **GREAT** STEP

TOWARDS

CONTROL

OF THE

MIND.

THE VALUE OF MEDITATION

One of my greatest passions in life is simple basic meditation. I have found that the key to meditation is quality breathing to quiet the mind and relax the body. When I first began meditating (many years ago) it was considered taboo by the general public, and even though we have advanced, those who don't understand the simplicity of it still shy away.

Today the mystery has been taken out of meditation and it can be very simple to understand. I personally believe one of the greatest gifts we can give ourselves in life is the art of meditation.

If you don't want to go to class there are some great guided meditation CDs and tapes available. These help immensely and can be a lot of fun, as well as helping us find peace and calm in the fast pace of modern day life.

The real value of attending class is the extra energy shared by like-minded people. Also most classes stay back these days and discuss their meditation journey and experiences. During these discussions we often find that someone has answered one or more questions we had in our own minds.

> *In our own circle over the years I have watched with delight some of our group helping each other grow and go forward.*

Another advantage is the beautiful friendships formed, even romances.

Meditation circles these days (some) are even social events where like-minded people feel free to be themselves.

Visit www.expandingenergies.com.au for Kawena's Guided Meditation CD's

<u>*MEDITATION*</u>

MEDITATION IS AN

*ACTIVITY OF <u>**"BEING"**</u> AND*

<u>**NOT**</u> *ONE OF <u>**"DOING"**</u>*

IT GIVES OUR

<u>**IMAGINATION**</u>

FULL REIGN OF

<u>**EXPRESSION**</u>

AS WE RELAX

THE BODY AND STILL THE

<u>**MIND.**</u>

IN GROUP MEDITATION
ESPECIALLY A CIRCLE,
WE ARE
CREATING AN ELECTRICAL
ENERGY FIELD
WHICH BECOMES A
CONNECTION
OF
PHYSICAL
MENTAL
AND
SPIRITUAL ENERGIES.

THIS IS THE IDEAL SITUATION
FOR
PERSONAL
OR
LONG DISTANCE
HEALING.

MEDITATION

Meditation isn't hard but it can be a little tricky.

My own experience of it is that if you try hard to meditate you never will.

Every now and then someone will come to me and say; "I try so hard to meditate but I can't." My answer always is, "Don't try at all, back off, focus on the breath and enjoy the soft back ground music."

Let the monkeys (your busy thoughts) run around in your mind till they get tired and give up when you don't try to stop them.

When I first learned to meditate I became so frustrated because I tried so hard but couldn't quite make it. After three months I decided to give up and at the last lesson thought to myself, "Just give up, relax and no more trying."

I just sat back, focused on the breath and listened to the music.

All of a sudden I heard in a distance our guide counting us back to the room.

I HAD DONE IT!

How happy was I. I had simply allowed meditation to come to me, and I don't think I have missed a day meditating since.

There are many ways to meditate and there is no right way, just whatever you feel compatible with is right for you.

I find this helps my beginner's classes:

Make yourself comfortable, back straight but relaxed, legs uncrossed, eyes looking straight ahead with your jaw pulled slightly back. Now very, very gently close your eyes.

Let your mind have its' way while it tries to organise future events like:

- What to cook for tea
- What to get at the supermarket
- What to say to little Jimmy when he is naughty.

Don't tell it to stop or it will fight you to the very end to keep control.

Just keep gently bringing your thoughts back to slow deep breathing then concentrate on hearing and feeling the music.

After a while the mind should give up and give you what you want which is quality meditation.

When following guided meditation it's ok to go off on your own visualising journey or even to the best sleep you'll ever have. The messages from your guide still go in subliminally. Your guide is mainly there to help you relax. It's really great to put on your peaceful music and sit or lie comfortably and use your own creative imagination to describe your quiet place.

- How it looks
- How it feels
- And how it sounds.

Use the words like calm, peaceful, quiet, harmony etc and you should have no trouble being your own meditation guide.

Now and then someone will say, "But I don't know if I'm really meditating or just telling myself a story" and yes you are.

The visual comes in when you describe something familiar with your creative thoughts.

The key word here is

'DESCRIBING.'

For instance instead of saying to yourself, 'I see a rose' say 'I see a beautiful deep red rose in full bloom with glossy, green leaves on the wooden table.'

You should see it quite clearly.

Try it with an old fashioned garden or describe the trees in your special forest.

We need to remember here we are dropping creative thoughts into the subby (subconscious mind).

If you are on your own right now put down the book and get comfortable, now gently close your eyes and describe in your own words:

- How beautiful that red rose is.

- How tall the trees in your quiet forest are.

- Or describe to yourself what you see in your old cottage garden.

As a rule once you start using your imagination the creative mind takes over and you are more likely to relax and enjoy the journey, especially if at first you do some slow, deep, quiet breathing. It might take a few times but again, don't try hard, be patient.

GROUP MEDITATION

It's a good idea to ask at least one or more good friends to join you.

Each one can take a turn to read these meditations softly and slowly.

OR

Buy a guided meditation CD and listen together.

It can even be something special to do when you get together for morning tea.

Maybe organise a meditation morning. Some of your friends would love it.

ANOTHER VERY SIMPLE, RELAXING MEDITATION TECHNIQUE.

If ever you become giddy, <u>stop</u> immediately.

In this exercise we will be breathing in through the nose and out through the mouth.

Sit or stand straight, shoulders dropped, head balanced.

Now take a long slow, deep breath to the count of seven, hold for the count of five and let go slowly and deeply to the count of seven.

<u>REST</u>

If you are on your own it is even better on the out breath to make a strong sound ha-a-a-a-a-a-a-a-a and when you hold the breath, think to yourself, "I am releasing all stress and tension, I am peaceful and calm."

Repeat just five or six times and you'll be amazed at how much lighter and more focused and relaxed you will be.

IN OUR

MEDITATIVE STATE

OUR IMAGINATION

HAS

UNLIMITED FREEDOM

OF

EXPRESSION.

EDGAR CAYCE

INTUITION

Follow the magic path of intuition.

- We need to listen to that still small voice inside us.

- Follow the hunch.

- Go with the gut feeling.

The path of the reasoning mind is much harder and slower and old habit patterns are hard to change.

We do have choices and negative thoughts will always defeat the heart's desire IF WE ALLOW THEM TO.

Always remember, every intuitive feeling is a sign post to happiness.

TRUSTING YOUR GUT FEELING

We need to always remember that our <u>gut feeling</u> is our own soul in action – guiding and directing us to all that is good and loving for us and those around us.

Our senses and feelings are the way our spirit and soul communicate with us on our human level. It is a way of warning us of danger and guidance to avoid trouble or making special positive decisions on our JOURNEY.

So to capture our own life's magic it requires our full constant awareness to keep our minds positive so we can draw towards us the UNIVERSAL guidance and direction.

This all simply means – keep your mind focused on the spirit within and positive thoughts. Build up your mental power by constantly trusting and loving God.

Love is the fulfilment of the universal law and faith is the power within, so trust your <u>senses and feelings to guide you forward.</u>

Many times in my early years I would look back and wish I had followed my intuition (sensing), as it would turn out I was mostly right.

It's a lot of fun testing your senses by playing guessing games. Some of us like to see how many times we can guess who is calling when the phone rings – or who is knocking at the front door – even who has sent us snail mail.

The big one is that quite often you think about someone, even after years have passed and the next thing you either see, hear from or about them. Spooky stuff, but, real just the same.

The secret to all this is keep an open mind and don't let the human side of you get in the way by creating doubts and fears in your mind and <u>trust that gut feeling</u>.

E.S.P

EXTRA SENSORY PERCEPTION

E.S.P involves perceiving through symbolism eg circles, squares, shapes, words, even one word, feelings, sense of smell or vision.

All these things are symbols to trigger your intuition so you can interpret their meanings on your own or others life path, we are all psychic but don't all practice it consciously.

We use our E.S.P unconsciously with hunches, gut feelings and sensing through our soul's awareness.

During sleep or meditation our psychic imagination has unlimited expression.

MEDITATION AND INFORMATION.

Much of my work and experiences have come from books and workshops.

A lot of it comes from meditation and relaxation, especially something new.

My favourite way of connecting with my angels and guides is at the end of my meditation. If I need any guidance or inspiration, it seems that while we are still in a calm, quiet situation they are happier to connect. It is well known these light energies don't come forward unless we are at peace or there is an urgent situation at hand.

I simply leave the music playing quietly at the end of meditation and if any messages do come through, I write them down as soon as possible.

There are many ways we can create a quiet space apart from meditating.

I sometimes sit at my window and gaze at the trees. You might like to sit in a park or on a quiet beach. Any peaceful spot will do. Just remember your pen and pad.

SIMPLE BASIC MEDITATION FOR BEGINNERS

The best advice I can give anyone is when they are listening to a new meditation CD, don't meditate at all the first time. Just sit quietly and listen to every word. Then when you are ready you will know what to expect.

If you fall asleep during meditation, don't worry, the subconscious does take it all in.

The second time just do the breathing exercises and listen to the music, but if your mind does start following your guide keep going but never try hard to do meditation, allow it to come to you.

It might take several times but keep on practicing.

Eventually when least expected you click in and you're there. <u>JUST BE PATIENT.</u>

It's always a good idea to take the phone off the hook and be as sure as you can there are no interruptions.

Also make sure your eyes are only VERY SOFTLY CLOSED.

WE DON'T CREATE STILLNESS.

STILLNESS IS ALWAYS THERE,

RIGHT AT THE CORE.

RIGHT FROM THE BEGINNING,

DEEP DOWN INSIDE.

WE JUST NEED TO ALLOW OURSELVES

PERMISSION TO MAKE THE CONNECTION.

BEING COMFORTABLE IN THE MEDITATIVE STATE

Lying down is fine as the spine automatically aligns itself.

When taking classes I like to let the students know to keep the spine straight but only as far as is comfortable. There's nothing worse than seeing someone sitting rigid as a ramrod, we must be relaxed to meditate successfully.

My favourite seat is an office chair – I advise everyone to get one even if they have no office.

"They are Magic"

You can have them high or low as you like. A small one is best. Just make sure you have one with a lumbar support. When sitting up it is also good to have your hands open and back into the creases of your thighs.

You'll find your wings (shoulders) automatically go back, the lungs open up and the breath flows in much easier.

The office chair in my opinion gives us greater comfort, support and relaxation.

For those who love to sit on the floor I advise you to invest in a meditation cushion. They are low at the front and higher at the back. With the buttocks being higher than the knees your spine is automatically aligned and comfortable.

HAPPY MEDITATING

Comfortable alignment is the key.

www.expandingenergies.com.au/audio_cds.html

Kawena's Meditation CD's for beginners and experienced:
*Meditation Made Easy
*Meditation Made Easy for Children

Chapter 7

Loving and Gifting

MOST OF US SPEND MUCH OF OUR LIVES THINKING OF THE PAST OR WORRYING ABOUT THE FUTURE THEN WE MISS OUT ON WHAT'S GOING ON IN THE PRESENT.

It's ok to think a little on the past and the future, but keep most of each day's 24 hours of energy to be as happy as you can on that day and tomorrow the same thing.

SELF CRITICISM IS THE WORST FORM OF MENTAL ABUSE.

Sounds pretty strong doesn't it? But it is true. It's bad enough when others criticise us but even worse when we do it to ourselves.

We are in our own company constantly. We are with ourselves twenty four hours a day, seven days a week and because of that we really need to be our own best friend, not our own worst enemy. Once we realise this, it makes sense that we take charge of what and how we think and gradually begin re programming our mind.

Self appreciation <u>is</u> the key to our subconscious mind in regards to our confidence and self esteem. We seem to find it easier to praise and encourage others more than ourselves, but unless we learn to lift our own spirit by at least mentally appreciating our own good qualities and <u>downgrading</u> our negative points, then we can't be of service in a truly loving way to either ourselves or others.

We are usually so quick to self criticise and it really only takes an instant to self destruct.

It's a good thing to treat everyone as an equal and to encourage them to be the best they can, but in future begin with yourself and soon you'll be a happier you.

RECLAIM YOUR LIFE
DON'T LIVE IN THE PAST,
IT'S TIME TO MOVE ON.

No matter what you have done wrong or who you have hurt,

THAT WAS THEN
THIS IS NOW
LET-IT-GO

Also don't let thoughts of a hurt from anyone keep on punishing you for the rest of your life.

If you do, they still have control over your emotions and your reaction to life. You repeatedly give them permission every time you re-enact that scene.

Every cell in the body reacts and the subconscious thinks it is what you want. So let's celebrate your decision to let-it-go. Always remembering, "We can only go as fast as our slowest wheel."

We need to let go of past hurts and condemnation, looking only for the positive, the love and the caring from this day on.

LETTING GO
THE **NEGATIVE PAST**
STAND UP!!
LOOK BEHIND *YOU!!*

Can you see the negative past with your eyes? Look.

Can you feel the negative past with your hands? Feel.

Can you taste the negative past with your mouth? Try.

NO? Then the past is no longer your reality.

They are just the negative pictures we look at with our mind's eye, wasting today's precious energy.

Be wise – practice living in today, we don't have power over the past any more. Make your mind up to lift your spirit to go forward to a happy future.

THE SECRET OF LOVE

is simply to do our best to be as kind as possible to ourselves and others. We do truly need to treat ourselves well before we can treat others well.

OUR TRUE WEALTH IS
THE GOOD WE DO IN
THE WORLD.

Practicing kindness acts is firstly for ourselves. It keeps the soul supple and the mind open and can also help others on their journey.

"THE ONLY JUSTIFICATION
FOR LOOKING DOWN ON
SOMEONE ELSE IS TO PICK
THEM UP."

Quote by Rev. Jesse Jackson

It is also time to open up our hearts, let the love flow and feel the love of Mother Nature as she envelopes us in her green leafy arms of life, living and loving.

THE POWER OF LOVE IS UNCONDITIONAL.

It soothes and heals all who welcome it.

We can only truly learn to love from the experience of the giving or sharing of our own-

- Love
- Enthusiasm
- Personality
- Soul
- Spirit
- Time
- and things

SO

✓ we embrace all of life

✓ we embrace all of people

✓ we embrace all of nature

Then we connect with the God spark within more than ever and wow! What a joy that becomes..

IT'S TIME –

we stood still and took a really good look at ourselves and how we each are created.

We need to realise that there have been millions of human beings living on Mother Earth and each one different.

ISN'T THAT AMAZING?
WE DO TAKE OUR HUMAN
BODY FOR GRANTED.

I guess that's because we are in it all our lives and it becomes a habit to almost ignore it as we rush around sometimes getting nowhere.

Let's think about this. Try standing still in front of the mirror no matter how plain or beautiful you may be.

Now take notice of your arms, legs, feet, toes, fingers, ears, eyes, nose, hair etc.

Now really concentrate and think about how incredible a creation we are and just think what a huge job our bodies have to do and the work that goes on inside is even more incredulous, everything is too organised not to be made to a

=MASTER PLAN=
Man himself can't make
a complete whole human
he might eventually
clone one
but
What about the Spirit?
What about the Soul?
He'll <u>never</u> do that one.

SO

It's time to stop taking ourselves for granted and truly value the greatness we are and also everyone else as well.

THE CREATOR
doesn't have to prove anything.

I AM the miracle

YOU ARE the miracle.

Let's get on with living and loving, knowing we don't have to know it all.

MORE MIRACLES

<u>Consider</u> the miracle of a full blown rose, waiting patiently for you to admire it.

<u>Consider</u> the miracle of a tall, beautiful, green tree, silhouetted against the evening summer sun.

<u>Consider</u> the miracle of a perfect orchid wafting its heavenly perfume across the gentle breeze.

<u>Consider</u> the miracle that nature (the universe) only creates one each of everything. It never duplicates anything. Every leaf, sometimes millions of them on a tree, have some tiny difference to each other.

It's time to get back to nature. She teaches us by example.

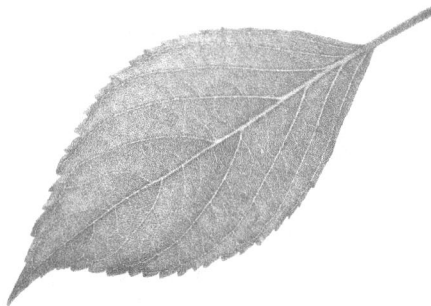

LOVE

IF WE WANT TO BE
LOVED
WE NEED TO
OPEN UP OUR
HEARTS
AND PUT OUR OWN
LOVE OUT THERE

SO

KARMA CAN MIRROR
IT BACK
TO US

IT'S BETTER TO SOMETIMES BE OPEN TO HURT, THAN TO CLOSE DOWN AND DIE INSIDE. I HAVE FOUND THAT SOME OF MY GREATEST LEARNING HAS COME FROM THE HURTS I HAVE RECEIVED.

THE

MORE

LOVE

WE

ALLOW

TO

FLOW

FROM

US

THE MORE IT **_FLOWS_**

BACK TO US.

LOVE
IS THE
FULFILMENT OF THE
__UNIVERSAL LAW__
AND
__FAITH__ IS THE
__ENERGY__ THAT OPENS
THE __CHANNEL__

A

PEACEFUL

HEART

IS

A

POWERFUL

HEART

LET'S FALL IN LOVE WITH MOTHER EARTH. WE INHERITED THIS AMAZING PLANET

AND ALL IT ASKS US TO DO IS TO

LOOK AFTER IT NURTURE IT PROTECT IT AND ENJOY IT.

A SMALL PRICE TO PAY FOR THE BEAUTY – THE SPLENDOUR AND THE EXCITEMENT IT CONTAINS. IT'S NOT ONLY THERE TO SUSTAIN US BUT TO SHOW US WHAT LIFE AND GROWTH TRULY ARE ALL ABOUT.

FALL IN LOVE
WITH THE
GOD SPARK
WITHIN
AND YOUR LIGHT
WILL SHINE
WITHOUT
AND YOU WILL
ATTRACT
LIKE MINDED,
WONDERFUL
PEOPLE INTO YOUR
LIFE

NOTHING

CAN

BRING YOU

THE GIFT OF PEACE

BUT

YOURSELF

Ralf Waldo Emerson

CREATE **FUN**
IN YOUR LIFE.

BE THE BEST!

ABSOLUTELY
THE BEST
PERSON YOU CAN
POSSIBLY BE

DARE TO BE **LARGER**
THAN LIFE

GET EXCITED ABOUT LIFE.

YOURS

THE MAGIC OF TEDDY BEARS

TEDDY BEARS
ARE
WONDERFUL THERAPY
WHENEVER YOU ARE SAD OR UNHAPPY

GO BUY YOURSELF
THE BIGGEST-
FATTEST-SOFTEST
TEDDY
YOU CAN AFFORD

Hugging a teddy creates a very calm, settling energy, and sometimes it is nice to give ourselves (or someone else) a little comic relief from the seriousness of everyday life.

I'm not sure why a teddy bear is so magical and approachable. Maybe it's because they've been around such a long time that we feel so familiar with them, then again it's possible they take us back to our childhood, and the memories connect us with the child within. I do know one thing:

THEY DON'T GOSSIP

THEY DON'T JUDGE US

THEY ARE TOTALLY LOYAL

THEY COST NOTHING TO KEEP

AND

THEY ARE <u>ALWAYS</u> THERE WHEN WE NEED A HUG.

I'd like to share a little story about my ex-husband (83yrs old). We've got past our past differences and become friends.

Just before Christmas he entered a low care nursing home. It is a lovely place with caring people looking after it. As we all know, it is very traumatic having to let go and settle into a new routine when a big change like this comes into your life.

I was at my wit's end how to be of help.

Then, I was doing my usual shopping and without realising it I found myself cuddling a large brown fluffy Christmas bear and couldn't put him down (I did try).

I have my own special bear so I knew it wasn't for me.

Then Les came into my mind and I argued with myself, he would think it so silly for an elderly man to have a teddy bear.

However without even thinking it through, I was at the checkout paying for him.

As it was, I had to visit Les next and still arguing with myself, automatically took Teddy, Santa hat and all, out of the car when I arrived at the nursing home.

YOU'VE GUESSED IT!!

When Ted and I walked into the room Les looked very down and sad but the minute he saw Ted his eyes lit up, he opened his arms and Teddy has lived on the bed in pride of position ever since.

Apparently Teddy is often the topic of conversation whenever carers or friends come into Les's room. Leslie says he even has conversations, in fun, with Ted and so do others.

Yep, I'm convinced teddy bears really do work their magic to help us be happy.

BE A HUGAHOLIC

It's wondrous what a hug can do,
A hug can cheer you when you're blue.
A hug can say, "I love you so,"
or
"Gee I hate to see you go,"

A hug is "Welcome back again,"
and
"Great to see you – where've you been?"

A hug can soothe a small child's pain,
And bring a rainbow after rain.
The hug!

There's just no doubt about it,
We scarcely could survive without it.
A hug delights and warms and charms,
It must be why God gave us arms.

Hugs are great for Dads and Mothers,
Sweet for sisters, swell for brothers.
And chances are, your favourite aunts
would love them more than potted plants.

Kittens crave them, puppies love them,
and heads of state are not above them.
A hug can break the language barrier
And make your travels so much merrier.

No need to fret about your store of 'em,
the more you give,
the more there's more of 'em.

So stretch your arms without delay
and give someone a hug today.

Author unknown.

This was given to me many years ago and I have lost count of how many times I have read it at classes.

IT'S A GREAT SPIRIT LIFTER.

BE
A
SPIRIT
LIFTER
LIFTING **OTHER PEOPLES**
SPIRITS AND
GIVING THEM BACK
THEIR **OWN SELF WORTH**
IS ONE OF THE MOST
VALUABLE THINGS WE CAN DO
WHILE WE ARE HERE
ON THE PLANET.
WHEN WE DO THIS
OUR OWN SELF WORTH
JUST G-R-O-W-S AND
G-R-O-W-S.

HAPPINESS

THE MORE WE

<u>HELP</u>

<u>OTHERS</u>

THE

<u>HAPPIER</u>

WE

BECOME.

SUCCESS

ONE

OF

THE

MOST

IMPORTANT RULES

OF

SUCCESSFUL LIVING

IS IN

SUCCESSFUL
GIVING.

GIVE
WITHOUT
RESERVATION
AND YOU WILL
RECEIVE
WITHOUT
RESERVATION.

The gift might not come back in similar form or from the same direction, but it will find it's way back eventually.

It is interesting to note that the first gift we receive is the touch of happiness that comes when we share with others.

A LITTLE BIT OF
PRAISE
GOES A LONG WAY.

PRAISE

IS ONE OF THE MOST

POWERFUL

FORMS OF GIVING, AND

ONE OF THE GREATEST

KARMIC ACTIONS.

Just one sincere word of praise from one human being can spur another onto great achievements. We all feel the need for a little acknowledgement. IT IS FOOD FOR THE SOUL.

GIFTS
THAT COST LITTLE CAN MEAN SO MUCH.

GIVE IN TO YOUR GIVING IMPULSES AS SOON AS POSSIBLE. DON'T WAIT TILL YOUR IMPULSE TO DO OR SAY SOMETHING HAS GONE.

DO IT NOW!!

If you are grateful to someone no matter how small the deed, let them know immediately and your spirit and theirs will both be lifted, otherwise the magic will disappear into infinity and be lost forever.

DON'T WAIT TILL YOUR LOVED ONES HAVE "POPPED OFF THE PLANET"

TELL THEM HOW MUCH YOU CARE OR REALLY LOVE THEM _NOW!_

GRAND EULOGIES AT A FUNERAL:

Help us and others heal and feel better.

But what about the dear departed? (ZILCH)

They've moved on, and how sad to think you never told them while they were here.

Maybe it's time to tell them before it's too late.

There is another old saying:

I'D RATHER YOU BRING ME ONE ROSE NOW, THAN A TRUCKLOAD WHEN I'M DEAD.

HAVE **FAITH**
IN ABUNDANCE
AND
GIVE
GIVE
GIVE

Be brave and open up your heart to give freely and joyfully with no expectations – just let it go.

The more we open our hearts to the world and it's people and animals the more our hearts expand to receive.

The secret to love – energy – happiness – even money lies in the giving.

THE LAW OF THE UNIVERSE RELIES ON THE BALANCE OF GIVING AND RECEIVING.

*HAVE THE COURAGE
TO
REACH OUT WHEN
YOU NEED **HELP**

REMEMBER HOW GOOD
YOU FEEL
WHEN **YOU** HELP
OTHERS?

WELL, ALLOW OTHERS
ACCESS TO THAT SAME
FEELING

BALANCE AND
UNDERSTANDING
COMES IN WHEN WE
LEARN TO RECEIVE AS
WELL AS GIVE*

___LIVING LIFE___
AND
___LOVING IT___
THE SECRET TO
HAPPY LIVING IS
___FREELY GIVING___

FIRST TO YOURSELF AND THEN TO OTHERS.

I have learned that the more you give, especially with no expectations, the more it comes back to you. Not particularly from where you gave, but it will find its way back.

The old saying, "It's greedy to ask for more than you need", is outmoded now simply because in asking for only enough for yourself you are limiting your ability to share with others.

GIVING

IS LIKE A

BOOMERANG

THE MORE YOU

GIVE IT AWAY

THE MORE IT COMES

BACK TO YOU

GIVING

THE
GREATEST
GIFT
WE CAN
GIVE _OTHERS IS_
HOPE _AND_ **_LOVE_**

THE SMALLEST
ACT OF KINDNESS
IS
WORTH FAR MORE
THAN
THE GREATEST OF
INTENTIONS

AUTHOR UNKNOWN

MAKE
GIVING
A FUN
THING

NOT ONLY WILL THE
SPIRIT *OF YOUR*
RECEIVER *BE HAPPY*

YOUR OWN **SPIRIT**
WILL BE LIFTED
AND DELIGHTED WITH
YOUR **ACHIEVEMENT**

ONCE WE DECIDE TO GIVE IN A HUGE
WAY IT'S AMAZING HOW EXCITING
LIFE BECOMES AND HOW MUCH
LIGHTER AND HAPPIER WE FEEL

SHARING

OURSELVES _WITH_

OTHERS _IS A_

HUGE _STEP_

TOWARDS

ACHIEVING

PEACE

WITHIN

What we share <u>mostly proves who we are.</u>

We are <u>constantly</u> sharing either the negatives or positives in our lives, we share either:

- Our misery or our happiness.

- Our joy or our sadness.

- Our conversation or our silence.

- Our peace or our aggression

ALSO:

our time, our love, our thoughts, our fears, our confidence, our experience etc.

WE NEVER STOP SHARING
BUT
WHAT WE CHOOSE TO SHARE
MOSTLY IS TRULY WHO WE BECOME

LIFE BECOMES SO
EXCITING
ONCE WE BEGIN TO
UNDERSTAND OURSELVES.

IT SEEMS ALL OF NATURE
BECOMES CLEARER AND WE
ALIGN WITH **MOTHER
EARTH** IN A MORE
KNOWING SENSITIVE WAY.

OUR SENSES BECOME
MORE ATTUNED TO
OTHERS NEEDS,
AND THOSE OF THE
EARTH.

A LITTLE BIT ON MANIFESTING

For the last forty to fifty years we have been thinking more and more about our things than ourselves.

There's nothing wrong with wanting lovely things to enjoy and share.

It's even great to want money so we can have a more comfortable and enjoyable life for ourselves and others to share.

I remember some people saying years ago, and some still do. "Money is the root of all evil."

THE <u>LOVE</u> OF MONEY IS THE ROOT OF ALL EVIL.

The word money is there to explain something that is simply the means of exchange.

The word manifesting is the latest fashion, we are hearing it everywhere.

We can manifest ABUNDANCE in many things, such as,

- Good health
- Wealth
- Wisdom
- Love
- Friends
- Things
- Knowledge etc etc

You might be interested in a couple of tips all in fun and worth a try.

Instead of cutting out pictures of other people's achievements (cars, houses etc) for your manifesting board, you might like to draw your own to put there.

If you are like me, not much of an artist, draw simple stick figures, keep it all in fun.

I feel that the personal touch helps to
DRAW WHAT YOU WANT TO YOU.

Another fun thing is to call your letterbox,
THE MONEY BOX

You never know, you might even find cheques as well as bills in there.
HAPPY MANIFESTING.

WHEN MANIFESTING

EACH ONE OF

US

IS

SPIRIT'S

CHANNEL

FOR

EACH OTHER.

QUOTES FROM MOTHER THERESA

"Charity is about LOVE, it isn't about pity. Charity and love are the same.

With charity you give love so don't only give money, reach out your hand as well.

The poor are hungry not only for food; they are hungry to be recognised as human beings. They are hungry for dignity and to be treated as we are treated.

THEY ARE HUNGRY FOR OUR LOVE."

"It's not how much you do but how much love you put into the doing and sharing with others that is important. Try not to judge people. If you judge others you are not giving them LOVE."

HELPING

CHARITY

IN A

PRACTICAL WAY

IS LIKE

PAYING RENT

ON THE SPACE

WE OCCUPY

WHILE WE ARE HERE

ON THE PLANET

SHARE YOUR
WINGS
WITH THOSE
WHO
HAVE TROUBLE
FLYING

GIVING
WITH
INTENTION

When we first start consciously working at giving and realise that the more we give, the more it comes back, we can't help thinking with the expectation of getting back what we put out.

So for a while we are really doing it

-WITH INTENTION-
THIS IS OK!

So don't feel guilty, because, after a while we do settle down into the rhythm of giving and receiving. We then find it such a joyous, happy feeling, we automatically do it:

WITHOUT THOUGHT OR
INTENTION THEN WOW!
WHAT A WONDERFUL LIFETIME HABIT
WE HAVE CREATED.

Chapter 8

My Grateful List

MY GRATEFUL LIST

I am grateful to still be alive.

I am grateful for my comfy bed.

I am grateful for my three great children, grandchildren and great grandchildren.

I am grateful I have plenty to eat.

I am grateful for this beautiful day.

I am also grateful I can read and write.

I am grateful I can still walk up and down stairs.

I am grateful for my excellent health.

I am truly grateful for so many wonderful friends.

I am grateful to still be able to work.

I am grateful to be able to still help others.

Etc – etc – etc – the list is endless.

THAT'S MY SHORT LIST, NOW HOW ABOUT YOU HAVING A GO?

APPRECIATION

Practice living in a world of appreciation of yourself and others.

Learn to look at your positive abilities as well as other people's positive abilities.

Redirect your thoughts from negative areas and search for the best in yourself.

When you do that you will automatically switch over to looking for the best in others.

"SEEK AND YOU WILL FIND"

Whether you are searching for the negative or the positive, that's definitely what you will find.

www.HappinessIsJustABreathAway.com

Chapter 9

Kawena's Summing Up

IN SUMMING UP

Be focused on quality breathing.

Raise your energy levels using many tools to achieve connection with the universe, such as – music, laughter, loving and giving, physical exercise, most of all meditation.

Work in with your angels/guides to connect with the energy you believe in.

Constantly following your dreams by trusting God, your intuition and your sensory abilities.

Expect no less than the best you can achieve by doing your best.

Create your own happiness and share your knowledge, talents and experiences with others.

Well Dear Reader

If you have stayed with me this far, you would realise by now, my main aim is to introduce you to the idea of, expanding your energies via breath power and the power of your mind.

I do hope you have enjoyed the read and learned something of value from our journey together.

Choose whatever modalities you resonate with to raise yourself to a higher ENERGY and VIBRATIONAL level.

Do it your way and above all, allow yourself to have LOTS of FUN, LAUGHTER and FRIENDS.

This alone will help you draw amazing excitement, vitality and enthusiasm into your life.

Thank you for joining me in flight.

So now it's time to put those beautiful "WINGS BACK TO GO FORWARD"

<u>YOU CAN DO IT</u>! If you think you can.
I wish you all the happiness your heart can possibly
hold.

Lovingly yours
Kawena.

MY FAVOURITE BOOKS

The Power of Positive Thinking
by Norman Vincent Peale
My first positive thinking book – there should be
one in every home.
http://normanvincentpeale.wwwhubs.com/

The Amazing Power of Deliberate Intention
by Esther and Jerry Hicks
(The Teachings of Abraham)
You need the best of guidance? Consider the
DVD's and CD's as well – you will be pleased you
did.
– www.abraham-hicks.com

From Elizabeth's and my point of view the
teachings of Abraham through Esther and Jerry
Hicks are amazing, straight-forward and easy to
understand

Reconnect with the Heart and Remember the Soul
by Elizabeth Joy
A beautiful book full of inspiring spiritual
guidance. Great for daily inspiration and
meditation.
– www.elizabethjoy.com.au

Ageless Body, Timeless Mind **by Deepak Chopra**
I value Deepak's practical spiritual writings partly
because like myself he promotes the power of the
breath to re-energise and revitalise mind-body-
soul.
www.chopra.com

How To Overcome Stress Naturally
by Tracey Stranger
Information and inspiration from experts and
everyday people to help you deal with stress
before the downward spiral into depression.
The breath is an important key.
www.HowToOvercomeStressNaturally.com

MORE FAVOURITE BOOKS

Think and Grow Rich Napoleon Hill

Miracle of The Breath Andy Caponigro

The Silva Mind Control Method Jose Silva

You Can Heal Your Life Louise L. Hay

Breathe For Life Sophie Gabriel

Instant Calm Paul Wilson

Meditation Pure and Simple Ian Gawler

The Mysteries of the Mind Edgar Cayce

How to Stop Worrying and Start Living Dale
Carnegie

The Angel Oracle - Cards and Book Ambika Wauters

Angels and Guides Kerry Edwards-Ticehurst

Angel Power Kerry Edwards-Ticehurst

Archangel Oracle Cards Doreen Virtue

The Lightworkers Way Doreen Virtue

The Reconnection Dr Eric Pearl

Living, Loving and Learning Leo F. Buscaglia

The 10 Day Turnaround Darren Stephens
www.the10dayturnaround.com

Our Internet Secrets Andrew & Daryl Grant
www.ourinternetsecrets.com

For more inspiration and motivation visit <u>www.expandingenergies.com.au</u>

Guided CD's, Sessions, Workshops by Kawena

<u>The Art of Breathing Made Easy CD</u>

Quality breathing helps supply the body with more oxygen which helps us to achieve a much better quality of life and our health will improve dramatically, especially the immune system.

<u>Meditation Made Easy CD</u>

Meditation can help in all areas of your life. From reducing stress and tension to becoming more creative and aware. My meditations are designed for both beginners and advanced.

<u>Meditation Made Easy For Children CD</u>

Suitable for 4yrs upwards in the style of storytelling so children can learn to visualise and use their imagination.

*<u>Private Session</u> - Life Direction
                     - Angel Card Readings

*<u>Private Mentoring and Motivation Session</u>

*<u>Workshops:</u> Happiness, High Energy & Motivation

ABOUT THE AUTHOR

Kawena (Gwen Gordon) is now 81 years young and a first time author showing you are never too old to live your dreams.

Born in NSW, Australia 1928 Kawena lived what may be called a normal life as wife and mother. It was always her dream as a little girl to sing and at the same time have a fascination in the power of the mind.

At 30 years of age the family moved to the Gold Coast in Queensland. Once the family grew up and moved out, Kawena learnt to sing at 45 years of age. Here she discovered the power of the breath and her whole life turned around being much more energised, motivated and confident than she had ever been.

Out went the old Gwen Gordon and in came Kawena.

Kawena spent the next 22 years singing up and down the Gold Coast with the Labrador Senior Citizens Group. Kawena also took her own singing group to nursing homes and other Senior Citizen venues.

Having experienced such joy and happiness in singing and understanding the importance of the breath, Kawena wanted to learn more about the power of quality breath.

Kawena constantly explored and studied the mind, the breath, meditation and different healing modalities such as sound & colour vibration, reiki and crystal healing and realised quality breathing was the key ingredient for high energy, happiness and motivation.

Kawena then moved from singing to teaching meditation and motivation in her regular meditation group plus High Energy Motivation workshops for the next 20 years.

Kawena enjoys the enthusiasm of the younger generation who are looking for purpose and direction, are keen to understand and improve their life, find their own happiness and have more energy. At the same time, teaching the 30 - 50 year old unemployed to be happy and motivated was immensely rewarding.

As Kawena followed her dreams, she now wants to share her story and motivate others to be happy and confident to follow their dreams.

Living on the beautiful Gold Coast in Queensland, Kawena's greatest joy in life is helping people understand what wonderful potential lies in each and every one of us and it doesn't matter how old or how young you are, you can always achieve your dream with the power of quality breathing and the power of the mind.

Most of this book is
a mini version of
Kawena's
Self Healing Workshops,
which she facilitates on the
Gold Coast,
Queensland. Australia.

Kawena
is also available for
Seminars
and as an
Inspirational Speaker.

SPECIAL FREE GIFT FROM KAWENA

2 for the price of 1
TICKETS TO KAWENA'S

Happiness - High Energy & Motivational Workshop
Gold Coast, Queensland

Total Value - INVALUABLE!

Be Uplifted - As she shares her world of wisdom and many practical secrets.

Be Ready - To share her love and laughter, and be truly inspired and motivated.

Go To www.expandingenergies.com.au
Enter your name & email address
Tick Workshop   ✔
Enter this code   **hhemw**
You will be emailed details of Kawena's upcoming workshops.

www.ingramcontent.com/pod-product-compliance
Lightning Source LLC
Chambersburg PA
CBHW060014100426
42740CB00010B/1488